WORLD HABITATS

WETLANDS

Rose Pipes

RSVP®

RAINTREE
STECK-VAUGHN
PUBLISHERS

The Steck-Vaughn Company

Austin, Texas

Published by Raintree Steck-Vaughn Publishers, an imprint of Steck-Vaughn Company

A ZOË BOOK

Editors: Kath Davies, Pam Wells
Design & Production: Sterling Associates
Map: Sterling Associates
Illustrations: David Hogg

Library of Congress Cataloging-in-Publication Data

Pipes, Rose.
     Wetlands / Rose Pipes.
         p. cm. — (World habitats)
     "A Zoë Book"—T.p. verso.
     Includes index.
     Summary: Introduces some notable wetlands around the world, including the Pantanal in Brazil, the Florida Everglades, and the Kakadu National Park in Australia.
     ISBN 0-8172-5001-8
     1. Wetlands—Juvenile literature. [1. Wetlands.] I. Title.
II. Series: Pipes, Rose. World habitats.
GB622.P56 1998
577.68—dc21

97-9072
CIP
AC

Printed in Italy
Bound in the United States
1 2 3 4 5 6 7 8 9   01 00 99 98 97

Photographic acknowledgments

The publishers wish to acknowledge, with thanks, the following photographic sources:

Environmental Images / Trevor Perry 26; Robert Harding Picture Library / M.H.Black - cover inset br; The Hutchison Library / Isabella Tree 7; Impact Photos / Dominic Sansoni - title page; / Piers Cavendish 12; / Maxine Hicks 21; / Neil Morrison 23, 25; / Brian Harris 27; NHPA / John Shaw 19; / Melvin Grey 28; / G.I.Bernard 29; Still Pictures / M Harvey - cover inset bl; / E.Robert/S.Bergerot 4; / Brecelj & Hodalic 9; / Mark Edwards 10; / Alain Pons 11; / Jorgen Schytte 13; / Roland Seitre 15; / Klein/Hubert 16; / Julio Etchart 17; Yves Lefevre / 20; TRIP / D Saunders 18; Woodfall Wild Images / Ted Mead - cover background, 22; Zefa 8, 24.

The publishers have made every effort to trace the copyright holders, but if they have inadvertently overlooked any, they will be pleased to make the necessary arrangement at the first opportunity.

Contents

All the words that appear in **bold** are explained in the Glossary on page 30.

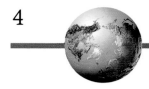

What Are Wetlands?

Wetlands are places where the ground is wet and soggy most of the time. Some wetlands are often flooded with water. They may be near rivers or near the sea. One of the largest freshwater wetlands in the world is in Africa.

The Okavango wetlands are in Botswana, Southern Africa.

Different types of wetlands have different names. They may be called marshes, swamps, bogs, **peat bogs**, or muskegs.

These pictures show some different types of wetlands and where they may be found.

peat bog

saltwater marsh

floodplain wetland

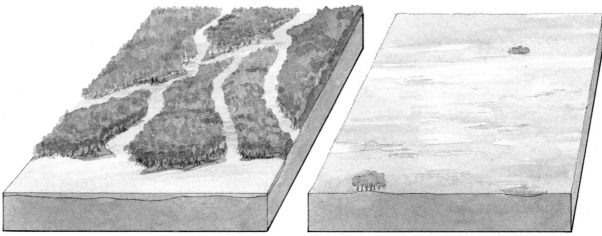

mangrove swamp

freshwater marsh

Where Are the World's Wetlands?

There are wetlands in most countries of the world. They may be in dry or wet places, and in hot or cold places. Some wetlands near the ocean are saltwater wetlands. Freshwater

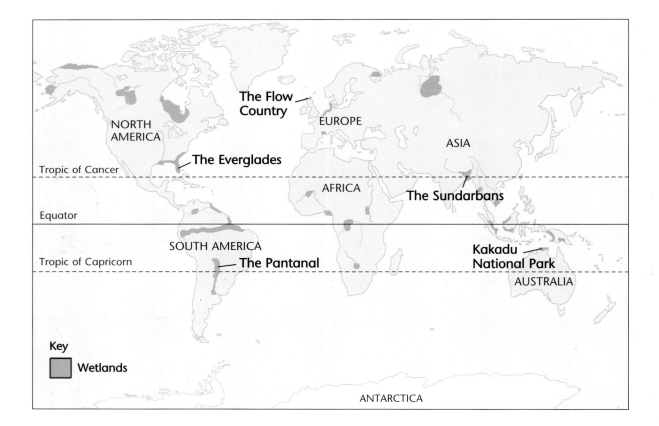

This map shows you where to find some of the largest wetlands in the world. Most wetlands are on low ground, but some are on high ground.

wetlands are often inland, close to rivers and lakes.

Different wetland **habitats** each have their own plants and animals. They are all **adapted** to living in wet places.

Waterbirds live in all wetlands. Some of the world's largest **mammals** live in wetlands, too. The rhinoceros is a large wetland mammal.

These animals are a kind of water antelope, called a lechwe. They feed on grass and live in wetlands in hot countries such as Botswana, Africa.

Using Wetlands

Grasses, stiff marsh plants called rushes, and reeds grow in wetlands. These plants are used to make all kinds of things, such as baskets, boats, and houses. People in Egypt

These are papyrus plants. They grow in wetlands in Africa. The ancient Egyptians used papyrus to make paper, as well as mats and sandals.

still use the papyrus plant to make everyday things, such as mats and baskets.

In some wetlands people go fishing, boating, and hunting. These activities may disturb or destroy the wetland habitat. Some wetlands are now **protected** from dangers like these.

People have drained many wetlands to make dry land for farming or for building towns and roads. This has destroyed the wetlands. The animals and plants that lived in these wetlands are gone forever.

This tin mine is in Thailand. Waste from the mine **pollutes**, or poisons, the water and kills wildlife in this wetland.

The Sundarbans in India and Bangladesh

There are hundreds of small channels, or creeks, in the Sundarbans. Most people who live in this region travel along the creeks by boat.

The Sundarbans wetland is partly in India and partly in Bangladesh. It is a forest wetland area, where three big rivers enter the Bay of Bengal.

The mangrove forest here is the largest in the world. Over forty kinds of mammals live in the Sundarbans.

Large mammals, such as the leopard, once lived in the forest. They have died out here because people hunted them. Leopard and tiger skins were highly prized. The tigers should be safe now because part of the forest is a tiger **preserve**.

The Bengal tiger is one of the largest mammals living in the Sundarbans. It is a good swimmer and hunter.

People who live in the Sundarbans get many of the things they need from the mangrove forest and the rivers. They are skilled at hunting and fishing.

The rivers are full of different kinds of fish. People catch fish to eat and to sell. They also hunt wild animals and gather plants from the forest.

People have cut down large areas of the mangrove forest for wood and to make farmland for growing rice. Clearing the forest brings problems and dangers.

The forest shelters the land from very strong ocean winds, called **cyclones**. If more trees are cut down, the cyclones will cause more damage.

Rice grows under water that comes from the rivers. These women are harvesting rice, an important food crop.

The Pantanal in Brazil

The Pantanal is the largest freshwater wetland in the world. It is in Brazil in South America. The Paraguay River runs through it. The river often floods the flat land all

The Pantanal is a patchwork of trees, lakes, and grasslands. There are few roads here, so people usually travel by boat.

around it. Only the higher ground stays dry.

The Pantanal is the most important habitat for waterbirds in South America. Birds stop here on their journey south from the Arctic lands in the north.

Many other wild creatures live here, such as the caiman and the capybara. The caiman is a kind of **reptile**. People hunt it for its skin. The capybara is the largest **rodent** in the world. It lives partly on land and partly in water. This animal eats grass.

The capybara's webbed feet help it to swim. The meat from the capybara is good to eat.

The rivers in the Pantanal often flood the flat land around them. People keep cattle on the dry grasslands that are too high for the floodwater to reach. Farmers plant grasses there for the cattle to eat. This changes the

Farmers want more land for cattle **ranches** like this one. They clear the trees and drain the wetlands. This destroys the wetland habitat.

habitat. Wild plants and animals lose their homes.

The rivers and lakes in the Pantanal are full of fish. Many people who live there catch the fish to eat and to sell.

Gold is mined in parts of the Pantanal. People use a metal called mercury in gold mining. Then they wash it away. The mercury **pollutes** the waters of the Pantanal, and many fish die. Mercury can poison humans, too.

The Pantanal is changing. People have built dams and **reservoirs** there. This picture shows an electrical power plant on the Paraná River.

The Everglades in Florida

The Everglades form a huge freshwater marsh in southern Florida in the United States. The marsh is an example of a wetland on low ground.

The Seminoles once lived in the Everglades. They called the marsh "grassy waters." This picture shows why this is a good name for the area.

In the rainy season, from June to October, Lake Okeechobee overflows and floods the Everglades. This lake is the largest lake in the South. It covers 700 square miles.

To the north of the marshes is the Big Cypress Swamp. Cypress trees grow here in the wet, swampy ground.

The cypress trees are adapted to living in the wet ground. They grow "knees" that are roots sticking up above the water to reach the air.

The grass that grows in the marshes is mostly saw grass. Its leaves have sharp edges with teeth, like the blade of a saw.

The shallow ponds in the marshes are called "gator holes" because the alligators make them. They scrape out the ground with their tails.

In the dry season, these "gator" ponds are the only wet places on the marshes. The fish,

Alligators live in the freshwater marshes of the Everglades.

birds, and other marshland animals need this water to stay alive.

The Everglades marshes are smaller now than they were when the Seminoles lived there. Half of the marshland was drained to make farmland and land for building towns.

A small part of the marsh is **preserved** in the Everglades **National Park**. People cannot drain this marsh or build on it.

People from nearby cities, such as Miami, like to see and enjoy the Everglades. They go boating and fishing there. Tourists visit from many other places, too.

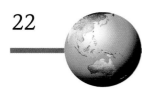

Kakadu National Park in Australia

Kakadu National Park is in a wetland near the north coast of Australia. Two rivers, the South and the West Alligator Rivers run through this wetland to reach the ocean.

This is a **billabong**, or freshwater pool, in Kakadu National Park. The Park is famous for its wildlife.

There are many different wetland habitats here. Near the coast there are **salt flats** and swamps. There are also freshwater marshes and pools, or billabongs. Different plants and animals live in each habitat. Some people go to the wetlands to fish and hunt for animals.

Wildlife is protected in Kakadu National Park. There are about 50 kinds of mammals, almost 1,000 kinds of plants, and 5,000 kinds of insects in the park.

Nearly 300 kinds of birds live in the park. Many of them, like the magpie geese in this picture, fly in huge flocks.

Aborigines have lived in the Kakadu area for more than 25,000 years. Today,

These Aborigines are gathering shellfish from this billabong in Kakadu.

Aborigines from other parts of Australia have come to live in Kakadu. Some still live by hunting, fishing, and gathering food. Others work on farms.

Thousands of tourists visit Kakadu Park every year. Most tourists go there to see the wildlife or to enjoy the beautiful beaches and scenery. Tourism has changed the wild habitat of the Kakadu wetlands. There are now roads and campsites in the park.

Twin Falls is a popular place for visitors. The best time to see the falls is in the wet season, from October to May.

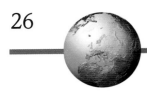

The Flow Country in Scotland

Cotton grass grows on peat bogs. You can see the fluffy white bolls of the cotton grass. They are like the pods or seedpods that grow on cotton plants.

There are many peat bogs in Great Britain. One of the largest is in the far north of Scotland. It is called the Flow Country. "Flow" means "marshy ground."

The Flow Country is a flat, windy area. It rains here most of the time, and the weather is usually cool. The winters can be very cold.

Peat is dead plant material that has partly rotted away. The peat is soggy when it is wet and hard when it is dry. When peat is cut and left to dry, it makes a very good fuel. Some people burn peat in fires and stoves in their homes.

People cut peat from the ground by making long trenches in the wetland.

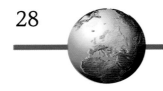

The plants that grow in peat are adapted to living in ground that is often wet. Mosses are just one example of plants that grow well in bogs.

Small lakes, or lochs, are scattered around

Many different kinds of birds live on the fish and plants in the lochs. The black-throated diver, shown in this picture, is often seen there.

the peat bogs. In fact, the bogs form in these shallow lakes.

Mosses, rushes, heather, and grass all grow in the peat. They provide food for the deer, rabbits, birds, and many other kinds of wildlife that live there.

The habitat in parts of the Flow Country changed when people began to plant trees in huge areas of the peat bogs.

Many people were upset and protested about the tree planting. They did not want the wildlife of the peat bogs to be destroyed. Now parts of the Flow Country are protected. No trees can be planted there, so the peat bog habitat is safe.

Purple heather grows between the rows of young fir trees planted on the peat bogs.

Glossary

Aborigine: The first people known to have lived in Australia.

adapted: If a plant or an animal can find everything it needs to live in a place, we say that it has adapted to that place. The animals can find food and shelter, and the plants have enough food in the soil and enough water. Some animals have changed their shape or their color over a long time, so that they can catch food or hide easily. Some plants in dry areas can store water in their stems or roots.

billabong: In Australia, the word billabong is used for a pool or water hole.

cyclones: A storm with strong winds that spiral, or turn in, toward the center. The cyclone brings heavy rain, too. A tornado is a type of smaller, stronger cyclone.

flood plain: Flat land that may be flooded.

habitat: The natural home of a plant or animal. Examples of habitats are deserts, forests, and wetlands.

mammals: The group of animals whose young feed on their mother's milk.

national parks: Laws are passed to protect these lands and their wildlife from harm. These places usually have beautiful scenery and rare wildlife.

peat bog: An area of wet, spongy ground made up of peat, a brown substance formed from dead plants.

pollutes: Makes dirty or very harmful. Polluted water contains waste materials. The waste may be poisonous and dangerous to wildlife.

preserve: An area of land set aside for wildlife to live in.

preserved: Saved or kept for the future. Preserved areas are kept safe from changes that would spoil or destroy them.

protected: Kept safe from changes that would damage the habitat.

ranches: Large farms where farmers keep cattle, sheep, or other animals.

reptile: One of a group of animals that includes snakes, lizards, and alligators.

reservoir: A lake that has been built to store water for people to use.

rodent: A kind of animal that has strong front teeth. Rats, mice, squirrels, and beavers are all examples of rodents.

salt flats: Flat land next to the sea or ocean that the salt water floods.

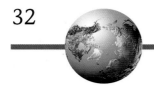

Index